SCHOLASTIC

GRAMMAR, SPELLING AND PUNCTUATION

SATs TESTS

YEAR 2

MSCHOLASTIC

Book End, Range Road, Witney, Oxfordshire, OX29 0YD

www.scholastic.co.uk

© 2018 Scholastic Ltd

123456789   8901234567

A British Library Cataloguing-in-Publication Data
A catalogue record for this book is available from the
British Library.

ISBN 978-1407-18293-3

Printed and bound by Ashford Colour Press

Author

Lesley Fletcher

Series consultants

Lesley and Graham Fletcher

Editorial team

Rachel Morgan, Tracey Cowell, Anna Hall,
Helen Lewis, Shelley Welsh, Jane Jackson, Liz Evans

Design team

Nicolle Thomas, Neil Salt and Oxford Designers and Illustrators

Illustrations

Garry Davies

Cover illustrations

Istock/calvindexter and Tomek.gr / Shutterstock/Visual Generation

Acknowledgements

Extracts from Department for Education website ©
Crown Copyright. Reproduced under the terms of the
Open Government Licence (OGL). www.nationalarchives.
gov.uk/doc/open-government-licence/version/3/

Every effort has been made to trace copyright holders
for the works reproduced in this publication, and the
publishers apologise or any inadvertent omissions.

Contents
Grammar, Punctuation & Spelling: Year 2

About this book

This book provides you with practice papers to help support children with end of Key Stage 1 Grammar, Punctuation & Spelling tests in school.

Using the practice papers

The practice papers in this book can be used as you would any other practice materials. The children will need to be familiar with specific test-focused skills, such as reading carefully, leaving questions until the end if they seem too difficult, working at a suitable pace and checking through their work.

About the tests

Each Grammar, Punctuation & Spelling test for Year 2 has two papers:

- a spelling task, lasting about 15 minutes (although this is untimed)
- a short-answer grammar, punctuation and vocabulary test, lasting about 20 minutes.

Neither of the papers should be strictly timed. You will need to ensure that children have enough time to demonstrate what they understand, know and can do, without prolonging the test inappropriately. Use your judgement to decide when, or if, children need breaks during the assessment, and whether to stop the test early if appropriate.

This book provides three different practice tests and the mark schemes as well as the script for the spelling tasks.

About Papers 1 and 2

Paper 1: Spelling task

This paper is made up of 20 target words contained in sentences.

Paper 2: Questions

In this paper, the children will need to be familiar with – and be able to demonstrate use of – grammar, punctuation and vocabulary content, including correct use and understanding of the terminology. See the test coverage table on page 6 for details of what they need to know.

Advice for parents and carers

How this book will help

This book will support your child to get ready for the Year 2 National Tests in Grammar, Punctuation & Spelling. It provides valuable practice of content expected of Year 2 children aged 6–7 years.

In the weeks leading up to the National Tests, your child may be given practice, revision and tips to give them the best possible chance to demonstrate their knowledge and understanding. It is helpful to try to practise outside of school and many children benefit from extra input. This book will help your child prepare and build their confidence.

In this book you will find three Grammar, Punctuation & Spelling tests. The layout and format of each test closely matches those used in the National Tests, so your child will become familiar with what to expect and get used to the style of the tests. There is a comprehensive answer section and guidance about how to mark the questions.

Tips

- Make sure that you allow your child to take the test in a quiet environment where they are not likely to be interrupted or distracted.
- Make sure your child has a flat surface to work on, with plenty of space to spread out and good light.
- Emphasise the importance of reading and re-reading a question.
- These papers are similar to the ones your child will take in May in Year 2 and they therefore give you a good idea of strengths and areas for development. When you have found areas that require some more practice, it is useful to go over these again and practise similar types of question with your child.
- Go through the tests again together, identify any gaps in learning and address any misconceptions or areas of misunderstanding. If you are unsure of anything yourself, then make an appointment to see your child's teacher who will be able to help and advise further.
- Practising little and often will enable your child to build up confidence and skills over a period of time.

Advice for children

What to do before the test

- Revise and practise regularly.
- Spend some time each week practising.
- Focus on the areas you are less sure of to get better.
- Get a good night's sleep and eat a healthy breakfast.
- Be on time for school.
- Have all the materials you need.

Test coverage table

Paper 2: Grammar, Punctuation & Vocabulary: Year 2

The children will need to be familiar with and be able to demonstrate use of the following.

	Content
Grammatical words and word classes	Nouns Verbs Adjectives Adverbs
Functions of sentences	Statements Questions Commands Exclamations
Combining words, phrases and clauses	Sentences
	Noun phrases
	Co-ordinating conjunctions Subordinating conjunctions
Verb tenses and consistency	Simple past and simple present tense Present and past progressive tense Tense consistency
Punctuation	Capital letters Full stops Question marks Exclamation marks
	Commas in lists
	Apostrophes for contraction Apostrophes for possession
Vocabulary	Prefixes Suffixes

About this paper

This paper tests your spelling.

There are **20 sentences**. A word is missing from each sentence. Your teacher, parent or carer will read out the missing word. They will also read out the whole sentence with the missing word in it. Write the missing word on the line in the sentence.

You will have about 15 minutes to complete the sentences.

You will be given up to 20 marks.

Grammar, Punctuation & Spelling

Test A, Paper 1: Spelling

1. Please close the _door._ _____.

2. We are using the bricks to build a _house_ _____.

3. She was playing with a _football_ _____ garage.

4. You need to feed a _anamal_ _____ every day.

5. There are lots of different types of _____ _colour_ _____.

6. Oscar's _____ has lots of train pictures.

7. He put on a warm _____ before going outside.

8. Check the baby's _____ isn't too hot.

9. The _____ were waiting to check in for their flight.

10. The _____ threw some nuts at us.

11. I can't _____ my school bag anywhere.

12. Put _____ pencil back in its pot.

13. She _____ the tree as far as the middle branches.

14. The flowers are _____ seeds onto the soil.

15. They were filled with _____ when the holiday ended.

16. My _____ take me for swimming lessons every week.

17. I _____ like to read that book after you.

18. I don't know _____ sent us that card.

19. The kittens _____ for their mother.

20. It was a _____ sunny day.

End of paper

Grammar, Punctuation & Spelling

Test A, Paper 2: Questions

About this paper

This paper tests your grammar, punctuation and vocabulary. There are different types of question to answer in different ways. Each question explains how to give the answer.

Read each question carefully. You will have about 20 minutes to complete the paper.

You will be given up to 20 marks.

Practice questions

a. Underline the **nouns** in the sentence below.

Josh kicked the ball into the net.

b. Circle the word that must start with a **capital letter**.

We were excited about our holiday to france.

Grammar, Punctuation & Spelling

Test A, Paper 2: Questions

1. In the table, write in full each of the words with an **apostrophe**.

The first one has been done for you.

Words with an apostrophe	Words in full
can't	cannot
isn't	
it's	

2. Draw lines to match each sentence with its correct type.

The first one has been done for you.

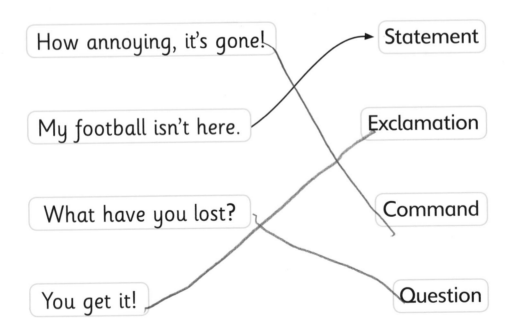

SCHOLASTIC National Curriculum SATs Tests

Marks

3. Circle the correct **verb** to complete this sentence.

I've _____ your football.

| find | found | finding |

1

4. Look at the football in the picture below.

Complete the **noun phrase** to describe the football.

the _____, _____ football

1

5. Write a different **joining word** in each space to complete the sentences below.

| but | and | because |

The children played football _____
it started to rain.

The rain stopped after about ten minutes
_____ they were able to play again.

1

6. Look where the arrow is pointing.

Jack scored a brilliant goal Ellie wasn't happy because he had cheated. ↑

Which **punctuation mark** is missing?

Tick **one**.

comma ☐

question mark ☐

full stop ☑

apostrophe ☐

Marks

1

---

7. Tick **two** sentences that are correct.

Tick **two**.

Ellie have lost her football. ☑

Jack helped Ellie to find it. ☑

They began playing football together. ☐

They goes indoors when it started to rain. ☐

1

Marks

8. Circle the correct word to complete the sentence.

We _was_ walking to school this morning.

| am | are | is | was |

1

9. I put my toys on the bottom <u>shelf</u> in the cupboard.
In the sentence above, what type of word is <u>shelf</u>?
Circle **one**.

| a noun | an adjective | a verb | an adverb |

1

10. Underline the **adjective** in the sentence below.

It was hard to walk on the frosty path.

1

1

Marks

11. Which sentence has the correct **punctuation**?

Tick **one**.

We brought some bread butter ham, and tomatoes for our sandwiches. ☐

We brought some bread butter, ham, and tomatoes for our sandwiches. ☐

We brought some bread butter, ham and tomatoes for our sandwiches. ☐

We brought some bread, butter, ham and tomatoes for our sandwiches. ☐

1

12. Draw lines to match each word to a **suffix** to make a new word.

You do not need to change any letters.

Words	Suffixes
sad	ment
harm	er
tall	ful
enjoy	ness

1

13. Underline the **adverb** in the sentence below.

Mrs Jones carefully counted all the children.

Marks

1

14. Choose the best **joining word** to complete the sentence. Write it in the space.

| when | if | that | but |

They began to drive home _____when_____ the storm started.

1

15. Write a **prefix** (word beginning) to make this word mean the opposite.

_____happy

1

Marks

16. Write the **past tense** of the verb <u>give</u> to complete the sentence.

| gives | given | gived | gave | gaved |

Ranvir _____ her friend some chocolate.

1

17. Write **s** or **es** to make each word a plural.

fox_____

frog_____

brush_____

1

18. Circle the two words that have missing **capital letters** in this sentence.

They went to london with oliver.

1

SCHOLASTIC National Curriculum SATs Tests

19. Josh wants to play football with Amy. Write what he will say to her, in the speech bubble. Remember to use correct punctuation.

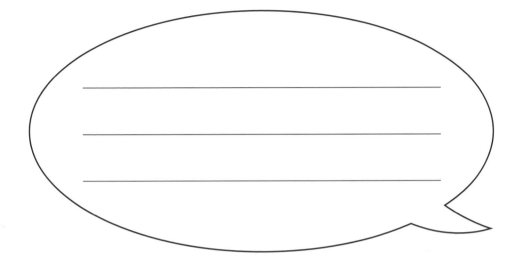

2

Test A: Marks

	Question	Focus	Possible marks	Actual marks
Paper 1	1–20	Spelling	20	
Paper 2	1	Punctuation: apostrophes for contraction	1	
	2	Grammar: sentence types	1	
	3	Grammar: tense consistency	1	
	4	Grammar: noun phrases	1	
	5	Grammar: conjunctions	1	
	6	Punctuation: full stops	1	
	7	Grammar: tense consistency	1	
	8	Grammar: present progressive	1	
	9	Grammar: nouns	1	
	10	Grammar: adjectives	1	
	11	Grammar: commas in lists	1	
	12	Vocabulary: suffixes	1	
	13	Grammar: adverbs	1	
	14	Grammar: conjunctions	1	
	15	Vocabulary: prefixes	1	
	16	Grammar: simple past tense	1	
	17	Vocabulary: plural suffixes	1	
	18	Grammar: capital letters	1	
	19	Grammar: questions Punctuation: question marks	2	
		Total	**40**	

SCHOLASTIC National Curriculum SATs Tests

About this paper

This paper tests your spelling.

There are **20 sentences**. A word is missing from each sentence. Your teacher, parent or carer will read out the missing word. They will also read out the whole sentence with the missing word in it. Write the missing word on the line in the sentence.

You will have about 15 minutes to complete the sentences.

You will be given up to 20 marks.

Test B, Paper 1: Spelling

1. My _____ starts at my shoulder and ends at my fingertips.

2. The _____ were very muddy after their walk.

3. I enjoy reading a _____ which has an exciting adventure.

4. A new _____ has started coming to our school.

5. The _____ station was very loud and busy.

6. We had to cross the _____ to get to the other side of the river.

7. Use a _____, so you can rub out any mistakes you may make.

8. We are getting a new slide in our _____.

9. I have been saving _____ to buy a new game.

10. The pirates buried the _____ in a dark cave.

11. There were many _____ animals in the safari park.

12. In history we have been learning about some

_____ men and women.

13. They _____ all the way round the lake.

14. The first _____ arrived at the finish line a few minutes before the rest of them.

15. I made _____ preparations for the camping trip.

16. My _____ supports our local football team.

17. He _____ see the blue sea in the distance.

18. A _____ one equals four quarters.

19. Mum bought me a new pair of _____ boots.

20. I had to go to _____ when I broke my leg.

End of paper

Grammar, Punctuation & Spelling

Test B, Paper 2: Questions

About this paper

This paper tests your grammar, punctuation and vocabulary. There are different types of question to answer in different ways. Each question explains how to give the answer.

Read each question carefully. You will have about 20 minutes to complete the paper.

You will be given up to 20 marks.

Practice questions

a. Underline the **adjectives** in this sentence.

The small red car was for sale.

---

b. Insert an **adverb** into the sentence below.

They _____ searched for the

missing toy.

Grammar, Punctuation & Spelling

Test B, Paper 2: Questions

1. Underline all the **nouns** in the sentence below.

The birds collect moss and twigs to make a nest.

1

2. They build the nest in <u>a safe place</u>.

What are the words <u>a safe place</u>?

Tick **one**.

A sentence ☐

A statement ☐

A noun phrase ☐

An adjective ☐

1

3. The sentence below has two mistakes. Write each **verb** correctly.

The birds **<u>lays</u>** their eggs and the mother bird **<u>sit</u>** on them to keep them warm.

1. _____

2. _____

1

SCHOLASTIC National Curriculum SATs Tests

Marks

4. Circle the correct **punctuation** for the end of this sentence.

When do you go on holiday

| ! | , | ? | . |

1

5. Look at the text in the box below. It is missing two **capital letters**.

Circle **two** words that must have a capital letter.

the new fledglings start to grow. the mother and father birds work hard to find them food.

1

6. Tick the best word or words to complete the sentence.

My mother is _____ than me.

Tick **one**.

old ☐

most old ☐

older ☐

oldest ☐

1

Marks

7. Write the correct **verb** to complete the sentence.

| has | had | have | having |

At first, most babies do not _____ any teeth.

1

8. Underline the **adverb** in this sentence.

The storm was raging noisily around the house.

1

9. Tick the answers that are **sentences**.

Tick **two**.

It was a very sunny ☐

The cat purred happily. ☐

always wanted a paddling pool. ☐

The ducklings followed the mother duck. ☐

1

Marks

10. Write the correct **verb** to complete the sentence below.

| is   are   was   were |

Mum lost her ring while she _____

walking the dog.

1

11. Draw lines to match each sentence with its correct type.

| What a disaster this is! | | Statement |

| Please can you help me? | | Exclamation |

| I need some help. | | Question |

| Help her. | | Command |

1

12. Tick the sentence that uses an **apostrophe** correctly.

Tick **one**.

The boys' bike was very muddy. ☐

The boy's bike was very muddy. ☐

The boys bike was' very muddy. ☐

The boys bike wa's very muddy. ☐

Marks

1

13. Draw lines to join each sentence to its correct end **punctuation**.

| I would like an ice cream | ? |

| Would you like an ice cream | ! |

| What a delicious ice cream this is | . |

1

14. Draw lines to join a word from each column to make a new word.

The first one has been done for you.

motor	shelf
sun	ball
book	bike
foot	shine

Marks

1

---

15. Tick the **sentences** that are correct.

Tick **two**.

The train are arriving at platform three. ☐

The bus is due in the village soon. ☐

We am waiting a long time. ☐

She is catching the bus this morning. ☐

1

16. Write the correct word to complete the sentence.

| paint | painted | painting | paints |

They were _____ a picture this afternoon.

Marks

1

17. What type of word is <u>wagged</u> in the sentence below?

The dog <u>wagged</u> his tail happily.

Tick **one.**

A noun ☐

A verb ☐

An adjective ☐

An adverb ☐

1

Marks

18. Which sentence must end with an **exclamation mark**?

Tick **one**.

What are you hoping to do at the theme park ☐

I wonder what you are doing ☐

What an exciting ride that was ☐

I didn't know what to do next ☐

1

19. What colour hair do you have?

Write an answer in the speech bubble. Use the correct punctuation.

2

End of paper

Test B: Marks

	Question	Focus	Possible marks	Actual marks
Paper 1	1–20	Spelling	20	
Paper 2	1	Grammar: nouns	1	
	2	Grammar: noun phrases	1	
	3	Grammar: tense consistency	1	
	4	Punctuation: question marks	1	
	5	Punctuation: capital letters	1	
	6	Vocabulary: suffixes	1	
	7	Grammar: tense consistency	1	
	8	Grammar: adverbs	1	
	9	Grammar: sentences	1	
	10	Grammar: past progressive	1	
	11	Grammar: sentence types	1	
	12	Punctuation: apostrophes for possession	1	
	13	Punctuation: full stops, question marks and exclamation marks	1	
	14	Vocabulary: suffixes	1	
	15	Grammar: tense consistency	1	
	16	Grammar: past progressive	1	
	17	Grammar: verbs	1	
	18	Grammar: exclamations	1	
	19	Grammar: statements Punctuation: capital letters and full stops	2	
		Total	**40**	

About this paper

This paper tests your spelling.

There are **20 sentences**. A word is missing from each sentence. Your teacher, parent or carer will read out the missing word. They will also read out the whole sentence with the missing word in it. Write the missing word on the line in the sentence.

You will have about 15 minutes to complete the sentences.

You will be given up to 20 marks.

Test C, Paper 1: Spelling

1. Jack won the _____ race at Sports Day.

2. The little _____ made a lovely bridesmaid.

3. A big _____ knocked us off our feet.

4. My grandma gave me a _____ of sweets.

5. The old _____ had a tall tower.

6. We went to a _____ match on Saturday.

7. I grew the tallest _____ in our class.

8. Ellie fell and hurt her _____.

9. Mum banged her _____ while she was playing tennis.

10. Dark black smoke came out of the _____.

11. We explored a very _____ castle.

12. After the test, our teacher gave us a _____ .

13. Please may I have _____ biscuit?

14. It was the _____ puppy in the litter.

15. We searched high and low, but it was _____ .

16. Louise hasn't _____ this game before.

17. Too much _____ is bad for you.

18. The _____ had a cake sale to raise money for charity.

19. Almost _____ knows how to ride a bike.

20. The train left the _____ on time.

End of paper

About this paper

This paper tests your grammar, punctuation and vocabulary. There are different types of question to answer in different ways. Each question explains how to give the answer.

Read each question carefully. You will have about 20 minutes to complete the paper.

You will be given up to 20 marks.

SCHOLASTIC National Curriculum SATs Tests

Practice questions

a. Circle the correct **punctuation** to end this sentence.

What an enormous elephant I saw

.   ,   ?   !

b. Write a **prefix** (word beginning) to make this word mean the opposite.

_____well

Marks

1. Come into our school!

The sentence above is:

Tick **one**.

a statement. ☐

a question. ☐

an exclamation. ☐

a command. ☐

1

2. Our school is in the pleasant village of delawood.

a. Find and **copy one** word that should start with a **capital letter**.

Word: _____

1

b. Look at the word you wrote above. Why should this word start with a capital letter?

Tick **one**.

It starts the sentence. ☐

It is the name of a place. ☐

It is the name of a month. ☐

It is the name of a person. ☐

1

Marks

3. Look at the sentence below. Circle the word that is missing a **capital letter**.

Every wednesday afternoon Year 2 have music and geography.

1

4. Put the missing **comma** in the correct place in the sentence below.

Year 2 have art music and geography today.

1

5. Write the best word to complete the sentence.

| has | have | having |

Our school _____ a uniform.

1

Marks

6. What type of word is <u>smart</u> in the sentence below?

We look very <u>smart</u> in our school uniform.

Circle **one**.

| a noun | a verb | an adjective | an adverb |

1

---

7. Choose the correct **punctuation** to end the sentence.

Did you know that we are also very successful, not just smart

Circle **one**.

| : | ? | ! | . |

1

8. Write the correct word to complete the sentence.

| when | and | that | or |

In autumn we enjoy going to a park

_____ has conkers.

Marks

1

9. Look at this picture.

Complete the **noun phrase** below to describe the treasure chest.

the _____ , _____

treasure chest

1

10. Which word correctly completes the sentence?

I was _____ home when it started to rain.

Tick **one**.

walk ☐

walked ☐

walks ☐

walking ☐

1

11. Write the correct word to complete the sentence.

| is | are | am | was | were |

I _____ going on holiday next week.

Marks

1

12. Tick one box in each row to match each sentence with the correct type.

Sentence	Statement	Question	Exclamation	Command
When are you going to play with me?				
I shall play with you when we have had tea.				
Play with me!				
How exciting this game is!				

1

13. Choose the best option to complete the sentence.

Mountains are _____ than hills.

Tick one.

high	☐
more high	☐
higher	☐
highest	☐

Marks

1

14. Write the best **joining word** to complete each sentence.

a. Today I had pizza for tea _____ Josh had pasta.

b. We couldn't have chips _____ we had no potatoes.

1

1

15. Circle the correct **suffix** to make a new word.

joy_____

ment	ful	ness	some

1

Marks

16. Complete the table below.

Singular	Plural
bird	
	books
wish	
	boxes

1

17. Tick one box in each row to show whether each sentence is in the **past tense** or the **present tense**.

Sentence	Past tense	Present tense
The wind was blowing the branches on the trees.		
There are many leaves on the path.		
The leaves floated down gently.		

1

18. Draw lines to match the words that have the same meaning.

One has been done for you.

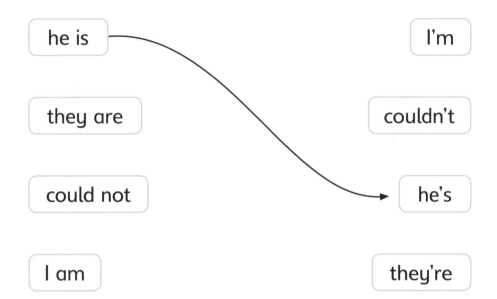

Marks

1

End of paper

Test C: Marks

	Question	Focus	Possible marks	Actual marks
Paper 1	1–20	Spelling	20	
Paper 2	1	Grammar: commands	1	
	2	Punctuation: capital letters	2	
	3	Punctuation: capital letters	1	
	4	Punctuation: commas	1	
	5	Grammar: simple present tense	1	
	6	Grammar: adjectives	1	
	7	Punctuation: question marks	1	
	8	Grammar: conjunctions	1	
	9	Grammar: noun phrases	1	
	10	Grammar: past progressive	1	
	11	Grammar: present progressive	1	
	12	Grammar: sentence types	1	
	13	Vocabulary: suffixes	1	
	14	Grammar: conjunctions	2	
	15	Vocabulary: suffixes	1	
	16	Vocabulary: plural suffixes	1	
	17	Grammar: simple past and present tense	1	
	18	Punctuation: apostrophes for contraction	1	
		Total	**40**	

Marking and assessing the papers

Grammar, punctuation, vocabulary and spelling, where appropriate in the tests, have right/wrong answers. However, there are some open-ended questions that require the children's input. For these questions, example answers have been provided. They are not exhaustive and alternatives may be appropriate, so careful marking and a certain degree of interpretation will be needed.

Marking paper 2: questions

Question type	Accept	Do not accept
Tick boxes	Clear, unambiguous marks.	Responses where more boxes have been ticked than required.
Circling or underlining	Clear, unambiguous indication of the correct answer – including a box.	Responses where more than the required number of words have been circled or underlined. Responses where the correct answer is circled or underlined, together with surrounding words. Answers in which less than half of the required word is circled or underlined.
Drawing lines	Lines that do not touch the boxes, provided the intention is clear.	Multiple lines drawn to or from the same box (unless a requirement of the question).
Labelling parts of speech	Clear labels, whether they use the full vocabulary required by the question or an unambiguous abbreviation.	Ambiguity in labelling.
Punctuation	Punctuation that is clear, unambiguous and recognisable as the required punctuation. mark.	Punctuation that is ambiguous, for example if it is unclear whether the mark is a comma or full stop.
Spelling	Where no specific mark scheme guidance is given, incorrect spellings of the correct response should be accepted.	Correct spelling is generally required for questions assessing contracted forms, plurals, verb. tenses, prefixes and suffixes.

Marking paper 1: spelling

- If more than one attempt is made, it must be clear which version the child wishes to be marked.

- Spellings can be written in upper or lower case, or a mixture of the two.

- If a word has been written with the correct sequence of letters but they have been separated into clearly divided components, with or without a dash, the mark should not be awarded.

- If a word has been written with the correct sequence of letters but an apostrophe or hyphen has been inserted, the mark should not be awarded.

- Any acceptable British-English spelling can be marked as correct. For example, *organise* or *organize*.

Marks table

At the end of each test there is a table for you to insert the number of marks achieved for each question. This will enable you to see which areas your child needs to practise further.

National standard in Grammar, Punctuation & Spelling

The mark that the child gets in the test paper will be known as the 'raw score' (for example, '38' in 38/40). The raw score will be converted to a scaled score and children achieving a scaled score of 100 or more will achieve the national standard in that subject. These 'scaled scores' enable results to be reported consistently year-on-year.

The guidance in the table below shows the marks that children need to achieve to reach the national standard. This should be treated as a guide only as the number of marks may vary. You can also find up-to-date information about scaled scores on our website: www.scholastic.co.uk/nationaltests

Marks achieved	Standard
0–23	Has not met the national standard in Grammar, Punctuation & Spelling for KS1
24–40	Has met the national standard in Grammar, Punctuation & Spelling for KS1

This spelling test can be found on pages 7–9.

Notes for conducting the spelling test

The task should take approximately **15 minutes** to complete, although you should allow children as much time as they need.

Read the instructions below to the children.

Listen carefully to the instructions I am going to give you.

I am going to read 20 sentences to you. Each sentence has a word missing. You should listen carefully to the missing word and fill this in, making sure you spell it correctly.

I will read the word, then the word within a sentence, then repeat the word a third time.

Do you have any questions?

Then read the spellings to the children as follows:

   1. Give the spelling number.

   2. Say 'The word is...'.

   3. Read the context sentence.

   4. Repeat 'The word is...'.

Leave at least a 12-second gap between spellings.

At the end, re-read all 20 questions. Then say *This is the end of the test please put down your pen or pencil.*

Each correct answer should be awarded **1 mark**.

For more information on marking this test, please refer to page 50.

Spelling one: the word is **door**.

Please close the **door**.

The word is **door**.

Spelling two: the word is **wall**.

We are using the bricks to build a **wall**.

The word is **wall**.

Spelling three: the word is **toy**.

She was playing with a **toy** garage.

The word is **toy**.

Spelling four: the word is **rabbit**.

You need to feed a **rabbit** every day.

The word is **rabbit**.

Spelling five: the word is **bread**.

There are lots of different types of **bread**.

The word is **bread**.

Spelling six: the word is **bedroom**.

Oscar's **bedroom** has lots of train pictures.

The word is **bedroom**.

Spelling seven: the word is **jacket**.

He put on a warm **jacket** before going outside.

The word is **jacket**.

Spelling eight: the word is **bottle**.

Check the baby's **bottle** isn't too hot.

The word is **bottle**.

Spelling nine: the word is **people**.

The **people** were waiting to check in for their flight.

The word is **people**.

Spelling ten: the word is **monkey**.

The **monkey** threw some nuts at us.

The word is **monkey**.

Spelling eleven: the word is **find**.

I can't **find** my school bag anywhere.

The word is **find**.

Spelling twelve: the word is **every**.

Put **every** pencil back in its pot.

The word is **every**.

Spelling thirteen: the word is **climbed**.

She **climbed** the tree as far as the middle branches.

The word is **climbed**.

Spelling fourteen: the word is **dropping**.

The flowers are **dropping** seeds onto the soil.

The word is **dropping**.

Spelling fifteen: the word is **sadness**.

They were filled with **sadness** when the holiday ended.

The word is **sadness**.

Spelling sixteen: the word is **parents**.

My **parents** take me for swimming lessons every week.

The word is **parents**.

Spelling seventeen: the word is **would**.

I **would** like to read that book after you.

The word is **would**.

Spelling eighteen: the word is **who**.

I don't know **who** sent us that card.

The word is **who**.

Spelling nineteen: the word is **cried**.

The kittens **cried** for their mother.

The word is **cried**.

Spelling twenty: the word is **beautiful**.

It was a **beautiful** sunny day.

The word is **beautiful**.

Q	Answers	Marks
	Practice questions **a.** <u>Josh</u> kicked the <u>ball</u> into the <u>net</u>. **b.** We were excited about our holiday to (france).	

1

Words with an apostrophe	Words in full
isn't	is not
it's	it is

Marks: 1

2

How annoying, it's gone! → Exclamation
My football isn't here. → Statement
What have you lost? → Question
You get it! → Command

Marks: 1

Q	Answers	Marks
3	found	1
4	Accept any appropriate noun phrase that includes two adjectives, such as the **old**, **muddy** football	1
5	The children played football **but** it started to rain. The rain stopped after about ten minutes **and** they were able to play again.	1
6	full stop	1
7	Jack helped Ellie to find it. They began playing football together.	1
8	are	1
9	a noun	1
10	frosty	1
11	We brought some bread, butter, ham and tomatoes for our sandwiches.	1

12

sad → ness
harm → ful
tall → er
enjoy → ment

Marks: 1

Q	Answers	Marks
13	carefully	1
14	when	1
15	**un**happy	1
16	gave	1
17	fox**es**, frog**s**, brush**es**	1

Q	Answers	Marks
18	They went to (london) with (oliver).	1
19	**2 marks** for appropriate question with capital letter and question mark. Accept any appropriate question, for example: Do you want to play football? **1 mark** for either an appropriate question or using a capital letter and question mark.	2
	Total	**20**

Test B, Paper 1:
Spelling test script and mark scheme

This spelling test can be found on pages 21–23.

Notes for conducting the spelling test

The task should take approximately **15 minutes** to complete, although you should allow children as much time as they need.

Read the instructions below to the children.

Listen carefully to the instructions I am going to give you.

I am going to read 20 sentences to you. Each sentence has a word missing. You should listen carefully to the missing word and fill this in, making sure you spell it correctly.

I will read the word, then the word within a sentence, then repeat the word a third time.

Do you have any questions?

Then read the spellings to the children as follows:

> **1.** Give the spelling number.
>
> **2.** Say 'The word is...'.
>
> **3.** Read the context sentence.
>
> **4.** Repeat 'The word is...'.

Leave at least a 12-second gap between spellings.

At the end, re-read all 20 questions. Then say *This is the end of the test please put down your pen or pencil.*

Each correct answer should be awarded **1 mark**.

For more information on marking this test, please refer to page 50.

Spelling one: the word is **arm**.

My **arm** starts at my shoulder and ends at my fingertips.

The word is **arm**.

Spelling two: the word is **dogs**.

The **dogs** were very muddy after their walk.

The word is **dogs**.

Spelling three: the word is **book**.

I enjoy reading a **book** which has an exciting adventure.

The word is **book**.

Spelling four: the word is **child**.

A new **child** has started coming to our school.

The word is **child**.

Spelling five: the word is **train**.

The **train** station was very loud and busy.

The word is **train**.

Spelling six: the word is **bridge**.

We had to cross the **bridge** to get to the other side of the river.

The word is **bridge**.

Spelling seven: the word is **pencil**.

Use a **pencil**, so you can rub out any mistakes you may make.

The word is **pencil**.

Spelling eight: the word is **playground**.

We are getting a new slide in our **playground**.

The word is **playground**.

Spelling nine: the word is **money**.

I have been saving **money** to buy a new game.

The word is **money**.

Spelling ten: the word is **treasure**.

The pirates buried the **treasure** in a dark cave.

The word is **treasure**.

Spelling eleven: the word is **wild**.

There were many **wild** animals in the safari park.

The word is **wild**.

Spelling twelve: the word is **great**.

In history we have been learning about some **great** men and women.

The word is **great**.

Spelling thirteen: the word is **walked**.

They **walked** all the way round the lake.

The word is **walked**.

Spelling fourteen: the word is **runner**.

The first **runner** arrived at the finish line a few minutes before the rest of them.

The word is **runner**.

Spelling fifteen: the word is **careful**.

I made **careful** preparations for the camping trip.

The word is **careful**.

Spelling sixteen: the word is **father**.

My **father** supports our local football team.

The word is **father**.

Spelling seventeen: the word is **could**.

He **could** see the blue sea in the distance.

The word is **could**.

Spelling eighteen: the word is **whole**.

A **whole** one equals four quarters.

The word is **whole**.

Spelling nineteen: the word is **hiking**.

Mum bought me a new pair of **hiking** boots.

The word is **hiking**.

Spelling twenty: the word is **hospital**.

I had to go to **hospital** when I broke my leg.

The word is **hospital**.

Test B, Paper 2: Questions mark scheme (pages 24–34)

Q	Answers	Marks
	Practice questions: **a.** The <u>small</u> <u>red</u> car was for sale. **b.** Accept any appropriate adverb, for example: carefully.	
1	The <u>birds</u> collect <u>moss</u> and <u>twigs</u> to make a <u>nest</u>.	1
2	A noun phrase	1
3	1. lay 2. sits	1
4	?	1
5	(the) new fledglings start to grow. (the) mother and father birds work hard to find them food.	1
6	older	1
7	have	1
8	noisily	1
9	The cat purred happily. **and** The ducklings followed the mother duck.	1
10	was	1
11	What a disaster this is! → Exclamation Please can you help me? → Question I need some help. → Statement Help her. → Command	1
12	The boy's bike was very muddy.	1
13	I would like an ice cream → . Would you like an ice cream → ? What a delicious ice cream this is → !	1
14	motor → bike sun → shine book → shelf foot → ball	1
15	The bus is due in the village soon. **and** She is catching the bus this morning.	1
16	painting	1
17	A verb	1
18	What an exciting ride that was	1
19	**2 marks** for an appropriate statement with capital letter and full stop. Accept any appropriate answer/statement, for example: My hair is brown. **1 mark** for an appropriate statement **or** using a capital letter and full stop.	2
	Total	**20**

Test C, Paper 1:
Spelling test script and mark scheme

This spelling test can be found on pages 35–37.

Notes for conducting the spelling test

The task should take approximately **15 minutes** to complete, although you should allow children as much time as they need.

Read the instructions below to the children.

Listen carefully to the instructions I am going to give you.

I am going to read 20 sentences to you. Each sentence has a word missing. You should listen carefully to the missing word and fill this in, making sure you spell it correctly.

I will read the word, then the word within a sentence, then repeat the word a third time.

Do you have any questions?

Then read the spellings to the children as follows:

1. Give the spelling number.

2. Say 'The word is...'.

3. Read the context sentence.

4. Repeat 'The word is...'.

Leave at least a 12-second gap between spellings.

At the end, re-read all 20 questions. Then say *This is the end of the test please put down your pen or pencil.*

Each correct answer should be awarded **1 mark**.

For more information on marking this test, please refer to page 50.

Spelling one: the word is **sack**.

Jack won the **sack** race at Sports Day.

The word is **sack**.

Spelling two: the word is **girl**.

The little **girl** made a lovely bridesmaid.

The word is **girl**.

Spelling three: the word is **wave**.

A big **wave** knocked us off our feet.

The word is **wave**.

Spelling four: the word is **tube**.

My grandma gave me a **tube** of sweets.

The word is **tube**.

Spelling five: the word is **church**.

The old **church** had a tall tower.

The word is **church**.

Spelling six: the word is **football**.

We went to a **football** match on Saturday.

The word is **football**.

Spelling seven: the word is **plant**.

I grew the tallest **plant** in our class.

The word is **plant**.

Spelling eight: the word is **knee**.

Ellie fell and hurt her **knee**.

The word is **knee**.

Spelling nine: the word is **wrist**.

Mum banged her **wrist** while she was playing tennis.

The word is **wrist**.

Spelling ten: the word is **chimney**.

Dark black smoke came out of the **chimney**.

The word is **chimney**.

Spelling eleven: the word is **old**.

We explored a very **old** castle.

The word is **old**.

Spelling twelve: the word is **break**.

After the test, our teacher gave us a **break**.

The word is **break**.

Spelling thirteen: the word is **another**.

Please may I have **another** biscuit?

The word is **another**.

Spelling fourteen: the word is **fattest**.

It was the **fattest** puppy in the litter.

The word is **fattest**.

Spelling fifteen: the word is **hopeless**.

We searched high and low, but it was **hopeless**.

The word is **hopeless**.

Spelling sixteen: the word is **played**.

Louise hasn't **played** this game before.

The word is **played**.

Spelling seventeen: the word is **sugar**.

Too much **sugar** is bad for you.

The word is **sugar**.

Spelling eighteen: the word is **children**.

The **children** had a cake sale to raise money for charity.

The word is **children**.

Spelling nineteen: the word is **everybody**.

Almost **everybody** knows how to ride a bike.

The word is **everybody**.

Spelling twenty: the word is **station**.

The train left the **station** on time.

The word is **station**.

Q	Answers	Marks
	Practice questions **a.** ! **b. un**well	
1	a command	1
2	**a.** delawood	1
	b. It is the name of a place.	1
3	wednesday	1
4	Year 2 have art**,** music and geography today.	1
5	has	1
6	an adjective	1
7	?	1
8	that	1
9	Accept any appropriate noun phrase that includes two adjectives, such as the **shiny, full** treasure chest	1
10	walking	1
11	am	1

12	Sentence	Statement	Question	Exclamation	Command	1
	When are you going to play with me?		✔			
	I shall play with you when we have had tea.	✔				
	Play with me!				✔	
	How exciting this game is!			✔		

Q	Answers	Marks
13	higher	1
14	**a.** and/but	1
	b. because/as/since	1
15	joy**ful**	1

16	Singular	Plural	1
	bird	**birds**	
	book	books	
	wish	**wishes**	
	box	boxes	

Q	Answers	Marks

17

Sentence	Past tense	Present tense
The wind was blowing the branches on the trees.	✔	
There are many leaves on the path.		✔
The leaves floated down gently.	✔	

Marks: 1

18

he is → he's

they are → they're

could not → couldn't

I am → I'm

Marks: 1

| | **Total** | **20** |

📖SCHOLASTIC National Curriculum SATs Tests